Intro

Table of Contents

How sweet! Each of these original baby blankets is tastefully textured – on both sides! The heirloom-quality afghans are completely reversible, so there's no front or back. Post Stitches add beautiful details to all five designs, which are crocheted using light weight yarn. You'll have fun creating them all, knowing the little darlings in your life will love them, too!

Meet Barbara Shaffer

Barbara Shaffer enjoys organic gardening and cooking, but her favorite pastime is crochet! The California designer inherited her fondness for wielding a crochet hook from her great-grandmother.

Barbara says, "Lately, I've been busy sewing wedding quilts and baby quilts for my children and grandchildren. But I plan to continue creating more patterns so fellow crocheters can enjoy the art as I do!"

Besides dreaming up sweet baby blankets to crochet, Barbara also creates gorgeous full-size throws and afghans. Her latest Leisure Arts publication is #5583 *Hooded Scarves*, five pretty and practical fashion accessories for cool weather. To find all of Barbara's must-have pattern books, visit your local retailer or LeisureArts.com.

Melon Ripples

Shown on front cover.

◼◼◼◻ **INTERMEDIATE**

Finished Size: 28" x 44" (71 cm x 112 cm)

MATERIALS

Light Weight Yarn
  [5 ounces, 459 yards
  (141 grams, 420 meters) per skein]:
  Cream - 4 skeins
  Melon - 1 skein
  Yellow - 1 skein
Crochet hook, size E (3.5 mm) **or** size needed for
  gauge
Yarn needle

GAUGE: In pattern, 2 repeats = 5⅝" / 14.25 cm

Gauge Swatch: 5⅝" w x 5½" h (14.25 cm x 14 cm)
Ch 38.
Work Rows 1-15 of blanket.
Finish off.

Stitch Guide

V-STITCH *(abbreviated V-St)*
(Dc, ch 1, dc) in st or sp indicated. When instructed
to work in a V-St, work in the ch-1 sp.

FRONT POST DOUBLE CROCHET
  (abbreviated FPdc)
YO, insert hook from **front** to **back** around post of
st indicated *(Fig. 1, page 15)*, YO and pull up a loop
(3 loops on hook), (YO and draw through 2 loops on
hook) twice. Skip st behind FPdc.

BACK POST DOUBLE CROCHET
  (abbreviated BPdc)
YO, insert hook from **back** to **front** around post of
FPdc indicated *(Fig. 1, page 15)*, YO and pull up a
loop (3 loops on hook), (YO and draw through
2 loops on hook) twice. Skip st in front of BPdc.

Blanket

With Cream, ch 190.

Row 1: Dc in fourth ch from hook (**3 skipped chs coun
as first dc**) and in next 6 chs, work V-St in next ch, dc i
next 8 chs, ★ skip next 2 chs, dc in next 8 chs, work V-S
in next ch, dc in next 8 chs; repeat from ★ across:
10 V-Sts and 160 dc.

Row 2: Ch 3 (**counts as first dc, now and throughout**),
turn; (work FPdc around next dc, work BPdc around
next dc) 4 times, work V-St in next V-St, work BPdc
around next 8 dc, ★ skip next 2 sts, (work FPdc around
next dc, work BPdc around next dc) 4 times, work V-St
in next V-St, work BPdc around next 8 dc; repeat from
across to last dc, leave last dc unworked.

Row 3: Ch 3, turn; work BPdc around next 8 sts, work
V-St in next V-St, (work BPdc around next st, work
FPdc around next st) 4 times, ★ skip next 2 sts, work
BPdc around next 8 sts, work V-St in next V-St, (work
BPdc around next st, work FPdc around next st) 4
times; repeat from ★ across to last 2 sts, leave last 2 sts
unworked.

Row 4: Ch 3 (**counts as first dc, now and throughout**),
turn; (work FPdc around next st, work BPdc around ne
st) 4 times, work V-St in next V-St, work BPdc around
next 8 sts, ★ skip next 2 sts, (work FPdc around next st
work BPdc around next st) 4 times, work V-St in next
V-St, work BPdc around next 8 sts; repeat from ★ acros
to last 2 dc, leave last 2 dc unworked.

Row 5: Ch 3, turn; work BPdc around next 8 sts, work V-St in next V-St, (work BPdc around next st, work FPdc around next st) 4 times, ★ skip next 2 sts, work BPdc around next 8 sts, work V-St in next V-St, (work BPdc around next st, work FPdc around next st) 4 times; repeat from ★ across to last 2 sts, leave last 2 sts unworked.

Row 6: Ch 3, turn; dc in back loop of next 8 sts *(Fig. 3, page 15)*, work V-St in next V-St, dc in back loop of next 8 sts, ★ skip next 2 sts, dc in back loop next 8 sts, work V-St in next V-St, dc in back loop of next 8 sts; repeat from ★ across to last 2 sts, leave last 2 sts unworked.

Row 7: Repeat Row 4.

Rows 8-11: Repeat Rows 3-6.

Rows 12-15: Repeat Rows 4 and 5 twice.

Finish off.

Row 16: Turn work and join Melon with slip st in last st made; working in back loops of sts and chs, sc in next 8 sts, 3 sc in next ch, sc in next 8 sts, ★ skip next 2 sts, sc in next 8 sts, 3 sc in next ch, sc in next 8 sts; repeat from ★ across to last 2 sts, leave last 2 sts unworked.

Row 17: Ch 1, turn; skip first sc, working in back loops only, sc in next 8 sc, 3 sc in next sc, sc in next 8 sc, ★ skip next 2 sc, sc in next 8 sc, 3 sc in next sc, sc in next 8 sc; repeat from ★ across to last sc, leave last sc unworked; finish off.

Row 18: Turn work and join Yellow with slip st in last sc made; working in back loops only, sc in next 8 sc, 3 sc in next sc, sc in next 8 sc, ★ skip next 2 sc, sc in next 8 sc, 3 sc in next sc, sc in next 8 sc; repeat from ★ across to last sc, leave last sc unworked.

Row 19: Ch 1, turn; skip first sc, working in back loops only, sc in next 8 sc, 3 sc in next sc, sc in next 8 sc, ★ skip next 2 sc, sc in next 8 sc, 3 sc in next sc, sc in next 8 sc; repeat from ★ across to last sc, leave last sc unworked; finish off.

Row 20: Turn work; working in both loops, join Cream with slip st in last sc made; ch 3, (dc in next sc, ch 1, skip next sc) 4 times, 3 dc in next sc, (ch 1, skip next sc, dc in next sc) 4 times, ★ skip next 2 sc, (dc in next sc, ch 1, skip next sc) 4 times, 3 dc in next sc, (ch 1, skip next sc, dc in next sc) 4 times; repeat from ★ across to last sc, leave last sc unworked; finish off.

Row 21: Turn work and join Yellow with slip st in last st made; working in back loops of sts and chs, sc in next 8 sts, 3 sc in next dc, sc in next 8 sts, ★ skip next 2 dc, sc in next 8 sts, 3 sc in next dc, sc in next 8 sts; repeat from ★ across to last 2 dc, leave last 2 dc unworked.

Row 22: Ch 1, turn; skip first sc, working in back loops only, sc in next 8 sc, 3 sc in next sc, sc in next 8 sc, ★ skip next 2 sc, sc in next 8 sc, 3 sc in next sc, sc in next 8 sc; repeat from ★ across to last sc, leave last sc unworked; finish off.

Rows 23 and 24: With Melon, repeat Rows 18 and 19.

Row 25: Turn work; working in back loops only, join Cream with slip st in first sc; ch 3, dc in next 8 sc, work V-St in next sc, dc in next 8 sc, ★ skip next 2 sc, dc in next 8 sc, work V-St in next sc, dc in next 8 sc; repeat from ★ across to last sc, leave last sc unworked: 10 V-Sts and 161 dc.

Row 26: Ch 3, turn; (work FPdc around next st, work BPdc around next st) 4 times, work V-St in next V-St, work BPdc around next 8 sts, ★ skip next 2 sts, (work FPdc around next st, work BPdc around next st) 4 times, work V-St in next V-St, work BPdc around next 8 sts; repeat from ★ across to last 2 dc, leave last 2 dc unworked.

Rows 27-135: Repeat Rows 3-26, 4 times; then repeat Rows 3-15 once **more**.

Finish off.

Lovely Lilacs

Shown on back cover.

 INTERMEDIATE

Finished Size: 32½" x 44½" (82.5 cm x 113 cm)

MATERIALS
Light Weight Yarn 🧶 **3** LIGHT
    [5 ounces, 395 yards
    (141 grams, 361 meters) per skein]:
    Lavender - 4 skeins
    Off-White - 2 skeins
Crochet hook, size E (3.5 mm) **or** size needed for
    gauge
Yarn needle

GAUGE: In pattern, 5 Shells and 11 rows = 4" (10 cm)

Gauge Swatch: 4¼" w x 4" h (10.75 cm x 10 cm)
Ch 29.
Work Rows 1-11 of Blanket.
Finish off.

Stitch Guide

SHELL
(2 Dc, ch 1, 2 dc) in st or sp indicated.
FRONT POST DOUBLE CROCHET
    (abbreviated FPdc)
YO, insert hook from **front** to **back** around post of
st indicated *(Fig. 1, page 15)*, YO and pull up a loop
(3 loops on hook), (YO and draw through 2 loops on
hook) twice. Skip st behind FPdc.
BACK POST DOUBLE CROCHET
    (abbreviated BPdc)
YO, insert hook from **back** to **front** around post of
FPdc indicated *(Fig. 1, page 15)*, YO and pull up a
loop (3 loops on hook), (YO and draw through
2 loops on hook) twice. Skip st in front of BPdc.

Blanket

With Lavender, ch 154.

Row 1: Work Shell in sixth ch from hook, ★ skip next
4 chs, work Shell in next ch; repeat from ★ across to las
3 chs, skip next 2 chs, dc in last ch: 30 Shells and 2 dc.

Rows 2-4: Ch 3 **(counts as first dc, now and
throughout)**, turn; ★ work FPdc around next 2 sts, ch 1
skip next ch-1 sp, work BPdc around next 2 sts; repeat
from ★ across to last dc, dc in last dc.

Finish off.

Row 5: Turn work and join Off-White with slip st in las
st made; ch 3, work Shell in each ch-1 sp across, dc in
last dc; finish off.

Row 6: Turn work and join Lavender with slip st in last
st made; ch 3, work Shell in each ch-1 sp across, dc in
last dc.

Rows 7-9: Repeat Rows 2-4.

Finish off.

Rows 10-104: Repeat Rows 5-9, 19 times; do **not**
finish off.

dging

Rnd 1: Ch 1, turn; 2 sc in first dc, ch 2, skip next 2 sts, in next ch-1 sp, (ch 4, skip next 4 sts, sc in next -1 sp) across to last 3 sts, ch 2, skip next 2 sts, 3 sc in t dc; working in end of rows, (ch 4, skip next 2 rows, in next row) across to last 2 rows, ch 4, skip last ows; working in free loops of beginning ch *(Fig. 2b, ge 15)*, 3 sc in corner ch, ch 4, skip next 2 chs and ch at se of next Shell, (sc in next ch-4 sp, ch 4) across, 3 sc in rner ch; working in end of rows, (ch 4, skip next ows, sc in next row) across to last 2 rows, ch 4, skip t 2 rows, sc in same st as first sc; join with slip st to st sc: 129 ch-4 sps and 2 ch-2 sps.

Rd 2: Ch 3, 2 dc in same st, ch 1, skip next st and next , dc in next ch, ★ working in sts and in chs, (ch 1, skip xt st, dc in next st) across to center sc of next corner, 1, 3 dc in corner sc; repeat from ★ once **more**, ch 1, c in next st, ch 1, skip next st) across to center sc of xt corner, 3 dc in corner sc, (ch 1, skip next st, dc in xt st) across to center sc of next corner; join with p st to first dc, finish off: 330 ch-1 sps and 338 dc.

d 3: Turn work and join Off-White with slip st in any rner dc; ch 3, dc in same st, dc in each st and in each -1 sp around, working 3 dc in each corner dc, dc in me st as first dc; join with slip st to first dc: 676 dc.

d 4: Ch 3, turn; 2 dc in same st, work FPdc around xt dc, (work BPdc around next dc, work FPdc around xt dc) across to next corner dc, ★ 3 dc in corner dc, rk FPdc around next dc, (work BPdc around next dc, rk FPdc around next dc) across to next corner dc; peat from ★ around; join with slip st to first dc, ish off: 684 sts.

d 5: Turn work and join Lavender with slip st in any rner dc; ch 3, (dc, ch 1, 2 dc) in same st, ch 1, skip next (dc in next st, ch 1, skip next st) across to center dc of xt corner, ★ work Shell in corner dc, ch 1, skip next (dc in next st, ch 1, skip next st) across to center dc of xt corner; repeat from ★ around; join with slip st to st dc, finish off: 346 ch-1 sps and 354 dc.

Rnd 6: Turn work and join Off-White with slip st in any corner ch-1 sp; ch 3, dc in same sp, dc in each st and in each ch-1 sp around, working 3 dc in each corner ch-1 sp, dc in same st as first dc; join with slip st to first dc: 708 dc.

Rnd 7: Repeat Rnd 4: 716 sts.

Rnd 8: Turn work and join Lavender with slip st in any corner dc; ch 3, dc in same st, ch 1, skip next st, (dc in next st, ch 1, skip next st) across to center dc of next corner, ★ work Shell in corner dc, ch 1, skip next st, (dc in next st, ch 1, skip next st) across to center dc of next corner; repeat from ★ around, 2 dc in same st as first dc, ch 1; join with slip st to first dc: 362 ch-1 sps and 370 dc.

Rnd 9: Ch 3, turn; work Shell in first ch-1 sp, dc in each st and in ch around, working Shell in each corner ch-1 sp; join with slip st to first dc: 4 ch-1 sps and 748 dc.

Rnd 10: Turn; slip st in each st to first ch-1 sp, ch 3, work FPdc around next dc, (work BPdc around next dc, work FPdc around next dc) across to next corner ch-1 sp, ★ 3 dc in corner ch-1 sp, work FPdc around next dc, (work BPdc around next dc, work FPdc around next dc) across to next corner ch-1 sp; repeat from ★ around, 2 dc in same sp as first dc; join with slip st to first dc: 756 sts.

Rnd 11: Ch 1, turn; 5 sc in first dc, † ch 4, sc in fourth ch from hook, skip next st, (sc in next st, ch 4, sc in fourth ch from hook, skip next 2 sts) across to center dc of next corner, 5 sc in corner dc, ch 4, sc in fourth ch from hook, skip next st, (sc in next st, ch 4, sc in fourth ch from hook, skip next 2 sts) across to within 2 sc of center dc of next corner, sc in next st, ch 4, sc in fourth ch from hook, skip next st †, 5 sc in corner dc, repeat from † to † once; join with slip st to first sc, finish off.

Baby Bow Ties

 **INTERMEDIATE**

Finished Size: 34" x 48" (86.5 cm x 122 cm)

MATERIALS
Light Weight Yarn **3**
[3.5 ounces, 359 yards
(100 grams, 328 meters) per skein]: 6 skeins
Crochet hook, size H (5 mm) **or** size needed for
gauge
Yarn needle

GAUGE: In pattern, 18 sts and 11 rows = 4" / 10 cm

Gauge Swatch: 6" w x 4" h (15.25 cm x 10 cm)
Ch 29.
Work Rows 1-11 of Blanket.
Finish off.

Stitch Guide

FRONT POST DOUBLE CROCHET
(abbreviated FPdc)
YO, insert hook from **front** to **back** around post of
st indicated *(Fig. 1, page 15)*, YO and pull up a loop
(3 loops on hook), (YO and draw through 2 loops on
hook) twice. Skip st behind FPdc.

BACK POST DOUBLE CROCHET
(abbreviated BPdc)
YO, insert hook from **back** to **front** around post of
FPdc indicated *(Fig. 1, page 15)*, YO and pull up a
loop (3 loops on hook), (YO and draw through
2 loops on hook) twice. Skip st in front of BPdc.

Blanket is worked lengthwise.

Blanket

Ch 209.

Row 1: Dc in fourth ch from hook (**3 skipped chs coun**
as one dc) and in each ch across: 207 dc.

Row 2: Ch 3 (**counts as first dc, now and throughout**)
turn; work FPdc around next dc, work BPdc around ne
5 dc, work FPdc around next dc, ★ ch 5, skip next 5 dc,
sc in next dc, ch 5, skip next 5 dc, work FPdc around
next dc, work BPdc around next 5 dc, work FPdc aroun
next dc; repeat from ★ across to last dc, dc in last dc:
60 BPdc, 24 FPdc, 22 ch-5 sps, 11 sc and 2 dc.

Row 3: Ch 3, turn; ★ dc in next 7 sts, ch 5, sc in next sc
ch 5; repeat from ★ across to last 8 sts, dc in last 8 sts:
86 dc, 22 ch-5 sps, and 11 sc.

Row 4: Ch 3, turn; work FPdc around next dc, work
BPdc around next 5 dc, work FPdc around next dc,
★ ch 5, sc in next sc, ch 5, work FPdc around next dc,
work BPdc around next 5 dc, work FPdc around next d
repeat from ★ across to last dc, dc in last dc: 60 BPdc,
24 FPdc, 22 ch-5 sps, 11 sc and 2 dc.

Row 5: Ch 3, turn; dc in each st and in each ch across:
207 dc.

Rows 6 and 7: Ch 3, turn, dc in each dc across.

Row 8: Ch 3, turn; work FPdc around next dc, (work
BPdc around next dc, work FPdc around next dc) acros
to last dc, dc in last dc.

Rows 9 and 10: Ch 3, turn; dc in each st across.

Rows 11-86: Repeat Rows 2-10, 8 times, then repeat
Rows 2-5 once **more**; do **not** finish off.

Edging

Rnd 1: Ch 3, do **not** turn; 4 dc in same st; working in end of rows, 2 dc in each row across to beginning ch; working in free loops of beginning ch *(Fig. 2b, page 15)*, 5 dc in first ch, dc in each ch across to next corner ch, 5 dc in corner ch; working in end of rows, 2 dc in each row across; working across last row, 5 dc in first dc, dc in next dc and in each dc across; join with slip st to first dc.

Rnd 2: Ch 1, work FPdc around same st, work BPdc around next dc, ★ work FPdc around next dc, work BPdc around next dc; repeat from ★ around; join with slip st to first st, finish off.

Pink Peaks

⬤⬤⬤◻ **INTERMEDIATE**

Finished Size: 32¼" x 51" (82 cm x 129.5 cm)

MATERIALS
Light Weight Yarn 🧶 **3** LIGHT
  [3 ounces, 279 yards
  (85 grams, 255 meters) per skein]: 10 skeins
Crochet hook, size C (2.75 mm) **or** size needed for
  gauge
Yarn needle

GAUGE: In pattern, 20 sts and 27 rows = 4" / 10 cm

Gauge Swatch: 5¾" w x 4" h (14.5 cm x 10 cm)
Ch 30.
Work Rows 1-27 of Blanket.
Finish off.

Stitch Guide

FRONT POST DOUBLE CROCHET
  (abbreviated FPdc)
YO, insert hook from **front** to **back** around post of
st indicated *(Fig. 1, page 15)*, YO and pull up a loop
(3 loops on hook), (YO and draw through 2 loops on
hook) twice. Skip st behind FPdc.

BACK POST DOUBLE CROCHET
  (abbreviated BPdc)
YO, insert hook from **back** to **front** around post of
FPdc indicated *(Fig. 1, page 15)*, YO and pull up a
loop (3 loops on hook), (YO and draw through
2 loops on hook) twice. Skip st in front of BPdc.

Blanket

Ch 150.

Row 1: Sc in second ch from hook and in each ch across
149 sc.

Work in back loops only throughout, unless instructed
otherwise *(Fig. 3, page 15)*.

Rows 2 and 3: Ch 1, turn; sc in each sc across.

Rows 4 and 5: Ch 1, turn; sc in first 4 sc, dc in free loop
of sc 2 rows **below** next st *(Fig. 2a, page 15)*, ★ sc in nex
9 sc, dc in free loop of sc 2 rows **below** next sc; repeat
from ★ across to last 4 sts, sc in last 4 sc: 15 dc and
134 sc.

Rows 6 and 7: Ch 1, turn; sc in first 3 sc, dc in free loop
of sc 2 rows **below** next sc, sc in next dc, dc in free loop
of sc 2 rows **below** next sc, ★ sc in next 7 sc, dc in free
loop of sc 2 rows **below** next sc, sc in next dc, dc in free
loop of sc 2 rows **below** next sc; repeat from ★ across to
last 3 sc, sc in last 3 sc: 30 dc and 119 sc.

Rows 8 and 9: Ch 1, turn; sc in first 2 sc, dc in free loop
of sc 2 rows **below** next sc, (sc in next dc, dc in free loop
of sc 2 rows **below** next sc) twice, ★ sc in next 5 sc, dc in
free loop of sc 2 rows **below** next sc, (sc in next dc, dc in
free loop of sc 2 rows **below** next sc) twice; repeat from
★ across to last 2 sc, sc in last 2 sc: 45 dc and 104 sc.

Rows 10 and 11: Ch 1, turn; sc in first 7 sts, dc in free
loop of sc 2 rows **below** next sc, (sc in next sc, dc in free
loop of sc 2 rows **below** next sc) twice, ★ sc in next 5 sts
dc in free loop of sc 2 rows **below** next sc, (sc in next sc
dc in free loop of sc 2 rows **below** next sc) twice; repeat
from ★ across to last 7 sts, sc in last 7 sts.

Building Blocks

Finished Size: 35½" x 37¾" (90 cm x 96 cm)

MATERIALS
  Light Weight Yarn
    [9.8 ounces, 893 yards
    (280 grams, 816 meters) per skein]: 2 skeins
  Crochet hook, size D (3.25 mm) **or** size needed for
    gauge
  Yarn needle

GAUGE: In pattern, 20 sts and 13 rows = 4" / 10 cm

Gauge Swatch: 4" square (10 cm)
Ch 22.
Row 1: Dc in fourth ch from hook (**3 skipped chs count as one dc**) and in each ch across: 20 dc.
Row 2: Ch 1, turn; sc in each dc across.
Row 3: Ch 3 (**counts as first dc**), turn; dc in next sc and in each sc across.
Rows 4-13: Repeat Rows 2 and 3, 5 times.
Finish off.

Stitch Guide

V-STITCH (*abbreviated V-St*)
(Dc, ch 3, dc) in st or sp indicated. When instructed work in a V-St, work in the ch-3 sp.
FRONT POST DOUBLE CROCHET
    (*abbreviated FPdc*)
YO, insert hook from **front** to **back** around post of st indicated (*Fig. 1, page 15*), YO and pull up a loop (3 loops on hook), (YO and draw through 2 loops on hook) twice. Skip st behind FPdc.
FRONT POST TREBLE CROCHET
    (*abbreviated FPtr*)
YO twice, insert hook from **front** to **back** around post of st indicated (*Fig. 1, page 15*), YO and pull up a loop (4 loops on hook), (YO and draw through 2 loops on hook) 3 times. Skip st behind FPtr.

Blanket

Ch 164.

Row 1: Dc in fourth ch from hook (**3 skipped chs count as one dc**) and in each ch across: 162 dc.

Row 2: Ch 3 (**counts as first dc, now and throughout**), turn; dc in next 7 sts, skip next 2 sts, work V-St in next st, skip next 2 sts, dc in next 4 sts, skip next 2 sts, work V-St in next st, skip next 2 sts, ★ dc in next 30 sts, skip next 2 sts, work V-St in next st, skip next 2 sts, dc in next 4 sts, skip next 2 sts, work V-St in next st, skip next 2 sts, repeat from ★ across to last 8 sts, dc in last 8 sts.

Instructions continued from page 8

Rows 12 and 13: Ch 1, turn; sc in first 8 sc, dc in free loop of sc 2 rows **below** next sc, sc in next dc, dc in free loop of sc 2 rows **below** next sc, ★ sc in next 7 sts, dc in free loop of sc 2 rows **below** next sc, sc in next dc, dc in free loop of sc 2 rows **below** next sc; repeat from ★ across to last 8 sts, sc in last 8 sts.

Rows 14 and 15: Ch 1, turn; sc in first 9 sts, ★ dc in free loop of sc 2 rows **below** next sc, sc in next 9 sts; repeat from ★ across.

Rows 16-19: Repeat Rows 4-7.

Rows 20 and 21: Repeat Rows 4 and 5.

Rows 22 and 23: Ch 1, turn; sc in each st across.

Rows 24-295: Repeat Rows 4-23, 13 times; then repeat Rows 4-15 once **more**.

Do **not** finish off.

Edging

Edging stitches are worked in **both** loops.

Rnd 1: Ch 3 (**counts as first dc, now and throughout**), turn; (dc, ch 2, 2 dc) in same st, ch 1, skip next st, (dc in next st, ch 1, skip next st) across to last st, (2 dc, ch 2, 2 sc) in last st; work 215 dc evenly spaced across end of rows to next corner; working in free loops of beginning ch (*Fig. 2b, page 15*), (2 dc, ch 2, 2 dc) in first ch, ch 1, skip next ch, (dc in next ch, ch 1, skip next ch) across to last ch, (2 dc, ch 2, 2 dc) in last ch; work 215 dc evenly spaced across end of rows to next corner; join with slip to first dc.

Rnd 2: Slip st in next dc and in corner ch-2 sp, ch 3, (dc, ch 2, 2 dc) in same sp, working in sts and in chs, dc in each st and in each ch across to next corner ch-2 sp, ★ (2 dc, ch 2, 2 dc) in corner ch-2 sp, dc in each st across to next corner ch-2 sp; repeat from ★ 2 times **more**; join with slip st to first dc.

Rnd 3: Ch 3, turn; dc in each dc around, working (2 dc, ch 2, 2 dc) in each corner ch-2 sp; join with slip st to first dc.

Rnd 4: Ch 1, turn; work FPdc around first dc, work BPdc around next dc, 2 sc in corner ch-2 sp, ch 3, sc in third ch from hook, 2 sc in same sp, ★ work BPdc around next dc, (work FPdc around next dc, work BPdc around next dc) across to next corner ch-2 sp, sc in corner ch-2 sp, ch 3, sc in third ch from hook, 2 sc in same sp; repeat from ★ 2 times **more**, work BPdc around next dc, (work FPdc around next dc, work BPdc around next dc) across; join with slip st to first st, finish off.

structions continued from page 10

Row 3: Ch 1, turn; sc in first 4 dc, skip next dc, work ?dc around next 3 dc, working in **front** of 3 sts just ?ade, work FPtr around skipped dc, (5 sc in next V-St, ?ip next 2 dc (last dc of V-St and next dc), work FPdc ?ound next 3 dc, working in **front** of 3 sts just made, ?rk FPtr around skipped dc) twice, ★ sc in next 22 dc, ?ip next dc, FPdc around next 3 dc, working in **front** ?3 sts just made, work FPtr around skipped dc, (5 sc in ?xt V-St, skip next 2 dc, work FPdc around next 3 dc, ?rking in **front** of 3 sts just made, work FPtr around ?ipped dc) twice; repeat from ★ across to last 4 dc, sc in ?t 4 dc.

Row 4: Ch 3, turn; dc in next 7 sts, skip next 2 sc, work ?St in next sc, skip next 2 sc, dc in next 4 sts, skip next ?c, work V-St in next sc, skip next 2 sc, ★ dc in next ?sts, skip next 2 sc, work V-St in next sc, skip next 2 sc, ?in next 4 sts, skip next 2 sc, work V-St in next sc, skip ?xt 2 sc; repeat from ★ across to last 8 sts, dc in last ?ts.

Rows 5-11: Repeat Rows 3 and 4, 3 times; then repeat ?w 3 once **more**.

Row 12: Ch 3, turn; dc in next 29 sts, ★ skip next 2 sc, ?rk V-St in next sc, skip next 2 sc, dc in next 4 sc, skip ?xt 2 sc, work V-St in next sc, skip next 2 sc, dc in next ?sts; repeat from ★ across.

Row 13: Ch 1, turn; sc in first 26 dc, skip next dc, work ?dc around next 3 dc, working in **front** of 3 sts just ?ade, work FPtr around skipped dc, (5 sc in next V-St, ?ip next 2 dc, work FPdc around next 3 dc, working in ?nt of 3 sts just made, work FPtr around skipped dc) ?ice, ★ sc in next 22 dc, skip next dc, work FPdc around ?xt 3 dc, working in **front** of 3 sts just made, work FPtr ?ound skipped dc, (5 sc in next V-St, skip next 2 dc, ?rk FPdc around next 3 dc, working in **front** of 3 sts ?st made, work FPtr around skipped dc) twice; repeat ?om ★ across to last 26 sts, sc in last 26 sts.

Rows 14-21: Repeat Rows 12 and 13, 4 times.

Rows 22-111: Repeat Rows 2-21, 4 times; then repeat Rows 2-11 once **more**.

Row 112: Ch 3, turn; dc in next sc and in each st across; do **not** finish off.

Edging

Rnd 1: Ch 4 (**counts as first dc plus ch 1, now and throughout**), turn; (dc, ch 1, dc) in same st, [skip next 2 dc, (dc, ch 1, dc) in next dc] across to last 2 dc, skip next dc, [dc, (ch 1, dc) twice] in last dc; working in end of rows, [(dc, ch 1, dc) in next row, skip next row] across to last 2 rows, (dc, ch 1, dc) in each of last 2 rows; working in free loops of beginning ch *(Fig. 2b, page 15)*, [dc, (ch 1, dc) twice] in first ch, [skip next 2 chs, (dc, ch 1, dc) in next ch] across to last 2 chs, skip next ch, [dc, (ch 1, dc) twice] in last ch; working in end of rows, (dc, ch 1, dc) in each of first 2 rows, [skip next row, (dc, ch 1, dc) in next row] across; join with slip st to first dc.

Rnd 2: Turn; slip st in first ch-1 sp, ch 4, dc in same sp, (dc, ch 1, dc) in each ch-1 sp and in each corner dc around; join with slip st to first dc.

Rnd 3: Turn; slip st in first ch-1 sp, ch 4, dc in same sp, [dc, (ch 1, dc) twice] in corner ch-1 sp, ★ (dc, ch 1, dc) in each ch-1 sp across to next corner ch-1 sp, [dc, (ch 1, dc) twice] in corner ch-1 sp; repeat from ★ 2 times more, (dc, ch 1, dc) in each ch-1 sp across; join with slip st to first dc.

Rnd 4: Turn; slip st in first ch-1 sp, ch 1, (sc, ch 3, sc) in same sp and in each ch-1 sp and corner dc around; join with slip st to first sc, finish off.

General Instructions

ABBREVIATIONS

BPdc	Back Post double crochet(s)
ch(s)	chain(s)
cm	centimeters
dc	double crochet(s)
FPdc	Front Post double crochet(s)
FPtr	Front Post treble crochet(s)
mm	millimeters
Rnd(s)	Round(s)
sc	single crochet(s)
sp(s)	space(s)
st(s)	stitch(es)
YO	yarn over

★ — work instructions following ★ as many **more** times as indicated in addition to the first time.

( ) or [ ] — work enclosed instructions **as many** times as specified by the number immediately following **or** work all enclosed instructions in the stitch or space indicated **or** contains explanatory remarks.

colon (:) — the numbers given after a colon at the end of a row or round denotes the number of stitches you should have on that row or round.

† to † — work all instructions from first † to second † **many** times as specified.

CROCHET TERMINOLOGY

UNITED STATES		INTERNATIONAL
slip stitch (slip st)	=	single crochet (sc)
single crochet (sc)	=	double crochet (dc)
half double crochet (hdc)	=	half treble crochet (htr)
double crochet (dc)	=	treble crochet(tr)
treble crochet (tr)	=	double treble crochet (dtr)
double treble crochet (dtr)	=	triple treble crochet (ttr)
triple treble crochet (tr tr)	=	quadruple treble crochet (qtr)
skip	=	miss

Yarn Weight Symbol & Names	LACE 0	SUPER FINE 1	FINE 2	LIGHT 3	MEDIUM 4	BULKY 5	SUPER BULKY 6
Type of Yarns in Category	Fingering, 10-count crochet thread	Sock, Fingering Baby	Sport, Baby	DK, Light Worsted	Worsted, Afghan, Aran	Chunky, Craft, Rug	Bulky, Roving
Crochet Gauge* Ranges in Single Crochet to 4" (10 cm)	32-42 double crochets**	21-32 sts	16-20 sts	12-17 sts	11-14 sts	8-11 sts	5-9 sts
Advised Hook Size Range	Steel*** 6,7,8 Regular hook B-1	B-1 to E-4	E-4 to 7	7 to I-9	I-9 to K-10.5	K-10.5 to M-13	M-13 and larger

*GUIDELINES ONLY: The chart above reflects the most commonly used gauges and hook sizes for specific yarn categories.

** Lace weight yarns are usually crocheted on larger-size hooks to create lacy openwork patterns. Accordingly, a gauge range is difficult to determine. Always follow the gauge stated in your pattern.

CROCHET HOOKS													
U.S.	B-1	C-2	D-3	E-4	F-5	G-6	H-8	I-9	J-10	K-10½	N	P	Q
Metric - mm	2.25	2.75	3.25	3.5	3.75	4	5	5.5	6	6.5	9	10	15

■□□□ BEGINNER	Projects for first-time crocheters using basic stitches. Minimal shaping.
■■□□ EASY	Projects using yarn with basic stitches, repetitive stitch patterns, simple color changes, and simple shaping and finishing.
■■■□ INTERMEDIATE	Projects using a variety of techniques, such as basic lace patterns or color patterns, mid-level shaping and finishing.
■■■■ EXPERIENCED	Projects with intricate stitch patterns, techniques and dimension, such as non-repeating patterns, multi-color techniques, fine threads, small hooks, detailed shaping and refined finishing.

AUGE

[ex]act gauge is **essential** for proper size. Before beginning [yo]ur project, make the sample swatch given in the [in]dividual instructions in the yarn and hook specified. [Af]ter completing the swatch, measure it, counting your [sti]tches and rounds carefully. If your swatch is larger or [sm]aller than specified, **make another, changing hook** [siz]e **to get the correct gauge**. Keep trying until you find [th]e size hook that will give you the specified gauge.

[PO]INTS

[As] in all crocheted pieces, good finishing techniques [m]ake a big difference in the quality of the piece. Make a [ha]bit of taking care of loose ends as you work. Thread a [ya]rn needle with the yarn end. With **wrong** side facing, [we]ave the needle through several stitches, then reverse [th]e direction and weave it back through several stitches. [W]hen ends are secure, clip them off close to work.

[P]OST STITCH

[W]ork around post of stitch indicated, inserting hook in [di]rection of arrow *(Fig. 1)*.

[Fi]g. 1

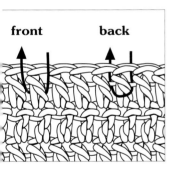

FREE LOOPS

After working in Back or Front Loops Only on a row or round, there will be a ridge of unused loops. These are called the free loops. Later, when instructed to work in the free loops of the same row or round, work in these loops *(Fig. 2a)*.

When instructed to work in free loops of a chain, work in loop indicated by arrow *(Fig. 2b)*.

Fig. 2a

Fig. 2b

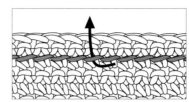
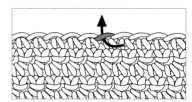

BACK OR FRONT LOOP ONLY

Work only in loop(s) indicated by arrow *(Fig. 3)*.

Fig. 3

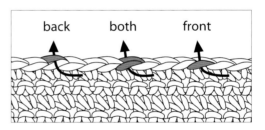

Yarn Information

The models in this leaflet were made using light weight yarn. Any brand of light weight yarn may be used. It is best to refer to the yardage/meters when determining how many balls or skeins to purchase. Remember, to achieve the same look, it is the weight of yarn that is important, not the brand of yarn.

For your convenience, listed below are the specific yarns used to create our photography models.

Melon Ripples

Lion Brand® Babysoft®
Cream - #099 Cream
Melon - #184 Melon
Yellow - #159 Lemon Drop

Lovely Lilacs

Bernat® Softee Baby®
Lavender - #30185 Soft Lilac
Off White - #30008 Antique White

Baby Bow Ties

Patons® Beehive Baby Sport
#09233 Spring Clover

Pink Peaks

Red Heart® Designer Sport™
#3730 Blush Rose

Building Block

Bernat® Baby Spor
#21302 Baby Deni Marl

We have made every effort to ensure that these instructions are accurate and complete. We cannot, however, be responsible for human error, typographical mistakes, or variations in individual work.

Instructions tested and photo models made by Janet Akins, JoAnn Bowling, Marianna Crowder, Dale Potter, and Margaret Taverner.

Production Team:
Technical Writer/Editor – Joan Beebe, Jean Guirguis, and Peggy Greig;
Editorial Writer - Susan McManus Johnson; Senior Graphic Artist - Lora Puls;
Graphic Artist - Dave Pope; Photography Manager - Katherine Laughlin;
Photo Stylist - Sondra Daniel; and Photographer - Ken West